Problem-Solving

TABLE OF CONTENTS 7B

Perimeter and Area

EXAMPLE

A backyard deck has the dimensions shown.

a. What length of fencing is needed to enclose the deck?

b. What area of wooden tiles will cover the deck?

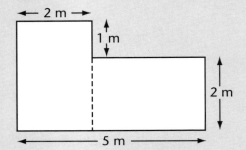

Solutions:

a. Perimeter : $2 + 1 + (5 - 2) + 2 + 5 + (2+1)$
    $= 2 + 1 + 3 + 2 + 5 + 3$
    $= 16$

Answer : 16 m of fencing is needed to enclose the deck.

b. Area : $2 \times (1 + 2) + (5 - 2) \times 2$
    $= 2 \times 3 + 3 \times 2$
    $= 12$

Answer : 12 m^2 of wooden tiles will cover the deck.

Solve the problems. Show your work.

① A flag is made up of 2 red rectangles with a white square in between containing a red star. Determine the area of each of the red rectangles in the flag shown.

1.4 m

3 m

Answer : _____

② 8 circles each having a diameter of 50 cm are drawn in a rectangle as shown. Calculate the area of the rectangle.

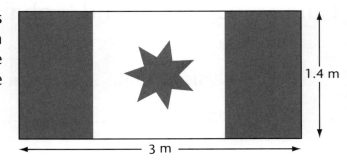

200 cm

50 cm

$L \times W = 100 + 200$
$= 20000 \ 100 \ cm$

Answer : _____

③ A walking group decides to do their 3-km walk around the base of the Toronto Dominion Bank Tower which measures 60 m by 36 m. How many times must they walk around the base of the tower in order to cover at least 3 km?

Answer : _____

④ A rectangular playground is to be constructed with an area of 16 m^2.

a. If the measurement is correct to the nearest 1 m, determine the different possible lengths of fence for enclosing the playground. (Remember a square is also a rectangle.)

Answer : _____

b. What is the minimum length of fencing you could use?

Answer : _____

⑤ The fence around a rectangular field measures 20 m.

a. If the measurement of each side is rounded to the nearest 1 m, determine the possible values for the area of the field.

Answer : _____

b. What is the difference between the maximum and minimum possible areas?

Answer : _____

c. What conclusion can you draw?

Answer : _____

⑥ An artist wants to make a mosaic picture with some small tiles. If the area of each tile is 1 cm^2 and the area of the picture is 1 m^2, how many tiles does the artist need?

Answer : _____

Study the diagrams carefully and solve the problems. Show your work.

Adam and Nadine have bought a house. The diagrams below show the dimensions of the backyard and the living room of their house.

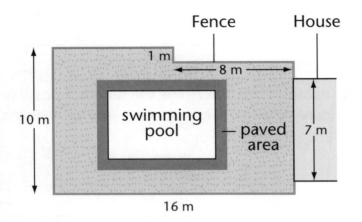

Backyard

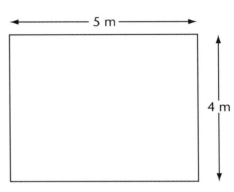

Ceiling: 2.5 m high

Living room

⑦ The backyard is enclosed by fencing which costs $15 /m. How much does the fencing cost?

Answer : _____

⑧ The swimming pool has dimensions of 5 m by 7 m. The paved area is 1 m wide. What is the area of the paved area?

Answer : _____

⑨ The backyard is planted with grass sod which costs $12 /m². What will the cost of the grass be?

Answer : _____

⑩ Adam and Nadine want to redecorate their living room. If the whole floor is to be carpeted and the carpeting costs $70 /m² including installation, determine the carpet cost.

Answer : _____

⑪ The walls and the ceiling of the living room are to be painted. The paint costs $8.99 /L and 1 litre covers 5 m². If the windows occupy 7 m², calculate the cost of the paint. (correct to the nearest cent)

Answer : _____

Solve the problems. Show your work.

⑫ The design on some traditional Canadian quilts is made up of parallelograms as shown. Determine the total area of the design.

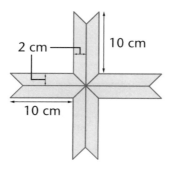

2 cm   10 cm

10 cm

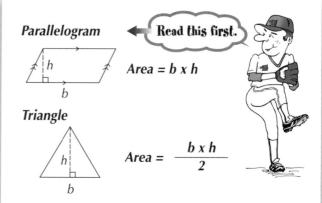

Parallelogram   ← Read this first.

Area = b x h

Triangle

Area = $\dfrac{b \times h}{2}$

- Congruent triangles have the same shape and size.
- An isosceles triangle has 2 sides equal.
- An equilateral triangle has 3 sides equal.

Answer : _____

⑬ 2 congruent equilateral triangles form parallelogram ABCD. The perimeter of each triangle is 24 cm. Determine the perimeter of the parallelogram.

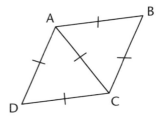

Answer : _____

⑭ Determine the average area of the three triangles drawn inside the given rectangle with dimensions of 9 cm × 4 cm.

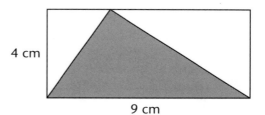

4 cm

9 cm

Answer : _____

⑮ A new corporate logo contains an isosceles triangle with sides 6 cm and 12 cm.

a. Determine the perimeter of the triangle.

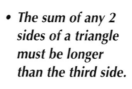

- The sum of any 2 ← Read this first.
  sides of a triangle
  must be longer
  than the third side.

Answer : _____

b. If the height of the triangle is 11.62 cm, determine its area.

Answer : _____

⑯ A hexagonal road sign has the dimensions shown.

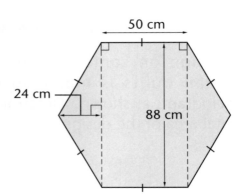

a.   Determine the perimeter of the sign.

Answer : _____

b.   Determine the area of the sign.

Answer : _____

⑰ Determine the shaded area if the area of each square is 1 cm².

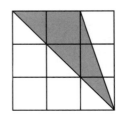

Answer : _____

⑱ A triangle with the base of 10 cm has the same area as a square with sides of 5 cm. Determine the height of the triangle.

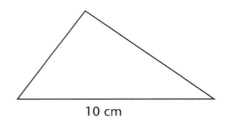

Answer : _____

⑲ Determine the area and the perimeter of the irregular shape.

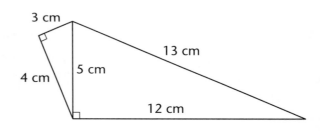

Answer : _____

⑳ The front of a farm shed has the dimensions shown. Determine the area.

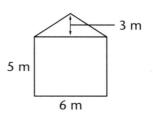

Answer : _____

㉑ The front and back of a blue box are trapezoidal in shape. Determine their total area.

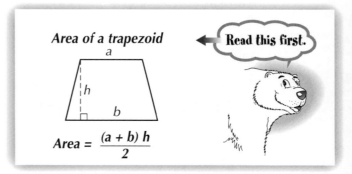

Answer : _____

㉒ The sides of the blue box are also trapezoids. Determine their total area.

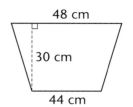
48 cm
30 cm
44 cm

Answer : _____

㉓ The given pattern is part of a quilt design made up of congruent triangles. Determine the total area of the shaded triangles.

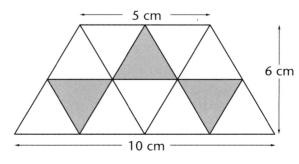
5 cm
6 cm
10 cm

Answer : _____

㉔ A carpet contains the hexagonal design shown. Determine the area of the shaded hexagon.

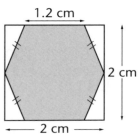
1.2 cm
2 cm
2 cm

Answer : _____

㉕ Suzie's doll house has dimensions as shown. Determine its cross-sectional area.

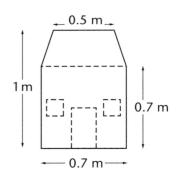
0.5 m
1 m
0.7 m
0.7 m

Answer : _____

CHALLENGE

A pentomino is a shape made up of 5 identical squares joined at their edges. Draw as many pentomino shapes as you can. Which pentomino has the smallest perimeter?

Answer : _____

UNIT 2 Volume and Surface Area

EXAMPLE

A tissue box has dimensions 12 cm by 22 cm by 7 cm.

a. How much cardboard is needed to make the box?

b. How much space does the box occupy?

Think :   The box is a rectangular prism.

Surface area = sum of the areas of 6 surfaces (2ab + 2bh + 2ah)

Volume   = area of base × height (a × b × h)

a. Surface area : $2 \times (7 \times 12) + 2 \times (12 \times 22) + 2 \times (7 \times 22)$

$$= 168 + 528 + 308$$

$$= 1004$$

Answer :   1004 cm² of carboard is needed.

b. Volume : $7 \times 12 \times 22 = 1848$

Answer :   The box occupies 1848 cm³.

Solve the problems. Show your work.

① How many cm³ are there in 1 m³?

Answer : _____

② How many cm² are there in 1 m²?

Answer : _____

③ A cube-shaped water container has dimensions 12 cm by 12 cm by 12 cm. How many litres of water can it contain?

Answer : _____

④ The total surface area of a cube is 54cm². What are the dimensions of the cube?

Answer : _____

For Question 1, ← **Read this first.**
1 m = 100 cm
1 m³ =100 cm x 100 cm x 100 cm

For Question 2,
1 m = 100 cm
1 m² =100 cm x 100 cm

For Question 3,
1 L = 1000 mL; 1 mL =1 cm³

⑤ The Riverview Emporium is located at the intersection of River Street and Main Street. Sketch diagrams to show how the building would look from

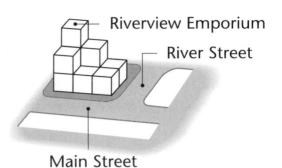
Riverview Emporium
River Street
Main Street

a. River Street.
b. Main Street.
c. a helicopter hovering over the building.

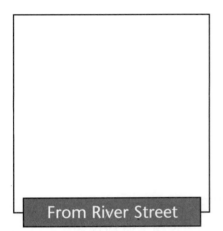
From River Street

From Main Street

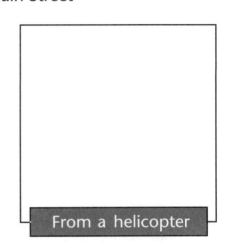
From a helicopter

⑥ The figure shown is made of 8 identical cubes. The cube marked k is removed. What effect does this have on the total surface area of the figure? Explain.

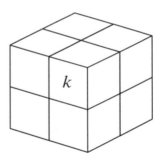

Answer : _____

⑦ The figure shown is made of 18 identical cubes, each having dimensions 2 cm by 2 cm by 2 cm.

a. If the cube marked x is removed, will the total surface area increase or decrease?

Answer : _____

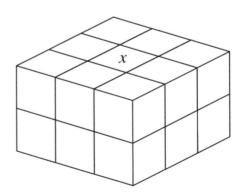

b. How many cm^2 will the surface area increase or decrease?

Answer : _____

⑧ Jill made a rectangular prism with tape, a pair of scissors and a piece of cardboard measuring 12 cm by 12 cm. Look how she cut and folded the cardboard to make the prism.

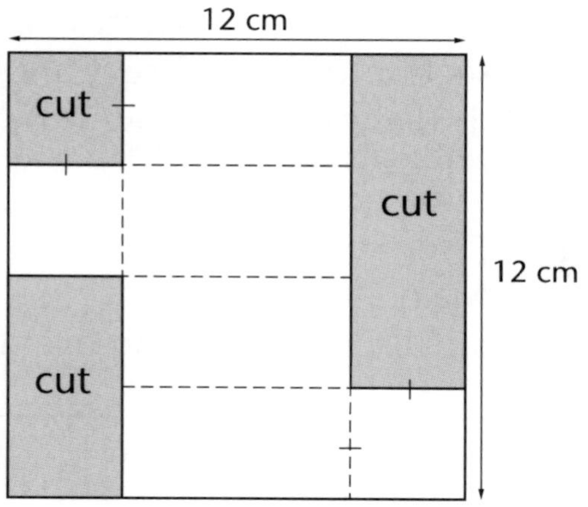

a. What are the dimensions of the prism?

Answer : _____

b. What is the total surface area of the prism?

Answer : _____

c. What is the volume of the prism?

Answer : _____

⑨ Jennifer wants to wrap a birthday gift for Anna. The dimensions of the box are 20 cm by 30 cm by 8 cm. Jennifer has a piece of 1 m² paper. Will she have enough paper?

Answer : _____

⑩ If you double each of the dimensions of a cube,

a. how does it affect the surface area?

Answer : _____

b. how does it affect the volume?

Answer : _____

⑪ The total surface area of a cube is 216 m². What is the volume of the cube?

Answer : _____

⑫ Bill constructed a wooden composter measuring 1.5 m by 1.2 m by 1 m.

   a. Determine the amount of wood required.

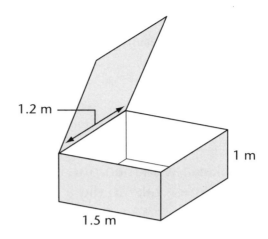

1.2 m

1 m

1.5 m

   Answer : _____

   b. Determine the volume of compost it can hold.

   Answer : _____

⑬ The dimensions of a room are 5 m by 4 m by 3 m. The area of the window on a wall is 3 m². If one 4 L can of paint can cover 36 m² and you want to paint the ceiling and the walls with 2 coats each, how many 4 L cans of paint do you need?

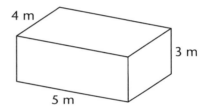

4 m

3 m

5 m

Answer : _____

⑭ How many dice each measuring 2 cm by 2 cm by 2 cm can be placed in a box of 10 cm by 10 cm by 10 cm?

Answer : _____

⑮ Ann has a collection of 50 hardcover books. 30 of the books have dimensions 16 cm by 23 cm by 3 cm and the other 20 books have dimensions 16 cm by 23 cm by 1.5 cm. What is the minimum volume of a container which will hold all these books?

Answer : _____

⑯ A box of laundry detergent (Box A) measuring 17 cm by 30 cm by 30 cm costs $11.99. Another box (Box B) measuring 15 cm by 25 cm by 25 cm costs $6.99. Which is a better buy? Explain.

Answer : _____

⑰ A cereal box measures 31 cm by 20 cm by 7 cm. It is completely filled with cereal. How many servings of cereal does it contain if each serving has a volume of 175 mL?

Answer : _____

⑱ It takes a workman one hour to dig a 3 m by 3 m by 3 m hole. How long would 2 workmen take to dig a 6 m by 6 m by 6 m hole at the same rate?

Answer : _____

⑲ The volume of the pyramid is $\frac{1}{3}$ of the volume of water in the rectangular tank. If the pyramid is submerged in the water, how high will the new water level be?

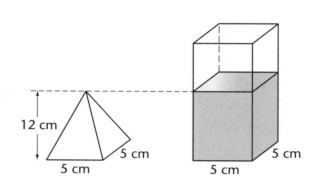

Answer : _____

⑳ The concrete steps leading to John's house have the dimensions shown. Determine the volume of cement needed to build the steps.

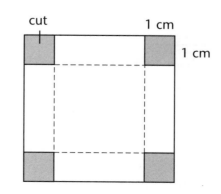

Answer : _____

㉑ A square piece of cardboard has an area of 25 cm². A shape of 1 cm² is cut from each corner. The sides are then folded to make an open box. What is the capacity of the box in mL?

Answer : _____

㉒ You are going to fill up the tank with tap water running at a rate of 20 L per minute. How long would it take?

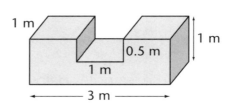

Answer : _____

㉓ A box measures 6 cm by 4 cm by 6 cm. All the surfaces of the box have been painted. The box is then cut up into cubes measuring 1 cm³. How many of these small cubes will have just one face painted?

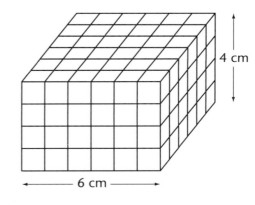

Answer : _____

CHALLENGE

Lennie tries to build different rectangular prisms with 12 1cm³ wooden cubes.

① Draw the different prisms he can build.

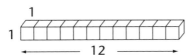

Answer : _____

② Calculate the surface area of each prism.

Answer : _____

③ Will the prisms have the same volume?

Answer : _____

Congruence and Similarity

EXAMPLE

Which of the triangles below are similar? Which are congruent?

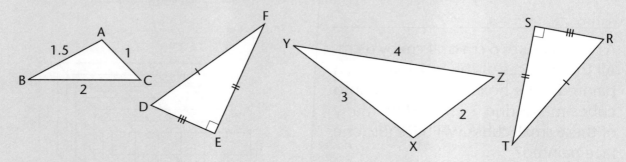

Answer :   △ABC and △XYZ are similar because their sides are proportional.

$$\frac{XZ}{AC} = \frac{XY}{AB} = \frac{YZ}{BC} \text{ i.e. } \frac{2}{1} = \frac{3}{1.5} = \frac{4}{2}$$

△DEF and △RST are congruent because they are equal in size and shape.

State whether these statements are true or false.

① If 2 figures are similar, they are also congruent.

Answer : _____

② 2 equilateral triangles are always similar.

Answer : _____

③ 2 rectangles of the same perimeter are always similar.

Answer : _____

④ If 2 figures are congruent, they are also similar.

Answer : _____

⑤ 2 squares with the same perimeter are congruent.

Answer : _____

⑥ A scale model of an object is similar to the object.

Answer : _____

- **2 figures are congruent if they are equal in size and shape.**
- **2 figures are similar if they have the same shape but not necessarily the same size. Their corresponding angles are equal and their corresponding sides are proportional.**

Read this first.

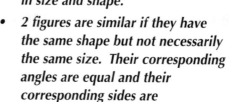

Solve the problems. Show your work.

⑦ An architect is drawing up the blueprint of Bill's house. The rectangular house has measurements 15 m by 18 m. If the scale of the blueprint is 1:300, determine the dimensions of the house on the blueprint.

Answer : _____

⑧ Bill has a rectangular swimming pool that measures 3 m by 7 m. Bob has a swimming pool that measures 3.6 m by 8.4 m. Are the two swimming pools similar? Give reasons to support your answer.

Answer : _____

⑨ There are 2 rectangular pictures on the wall of Bill's living room. One has dimensions 37 cm by 27 cm and the other, 26 cm by 21 cm. Are they similar? Explain.

Answer : _____

⑩ The main span of New York's Brooklyn Bridge is 540 m long. On a blueprint it measures 6 cm. What is the scale factor of the blueprint?

Answer : _____

⑪ Tom and Joe each construct a triangle with sides 4 cm , 5 cm and 6 cm. Will the triangles be congruent? Explain.

Answer : _____

⑫ 2 rectangular stamps are similar to each other. The smaller stamp has 2 sides of 2 cm and 2 sides of 1.2 cm. The larger stamp has 2 sides of 3 cm. Determine the length of the other 2 sides. (Hint: there are 2 possible values.)

Answer : _____

⑬ Jonathan's jean pockets are similar. Determine the side length of the larger pocket marked X.

Answer : _____

⑭ Two similar trapezoidal tents are erected. Determine the length marked X and the size of angle A.

Answer : _____

⑮ The sphinx is 20 m high and 14 m wide. If a scale model is made with a height of 9.6 cm, what should the width be?

Answer : _____

⑯ Are the 2 cars shown similar to each other? Explain.

Answer : _____

⑰ 2 rectangular pictures are hung side by side as shown. Are the pictures similar to each other? Explain.

Answer : _____

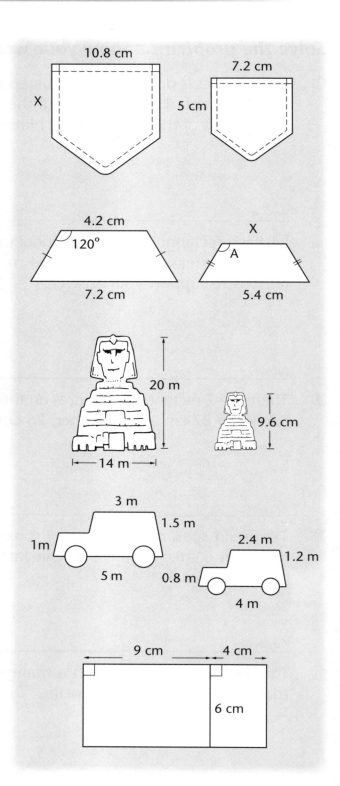

⑱ Ann and Betty each construct a triangle having angles 60°, 30° and 90°. Will the two triangles be congruent? Explain.

Answer : _____

⑲ An equilateral triangle has sides of 5 cm. Another equilateral triangle has sides of 4 cm. Are the triangles similar? Explain.

Answer : _____

⑳ Divide the shape into 4 congruent figures each of which is similar to the original shape. What is the area of each shape?

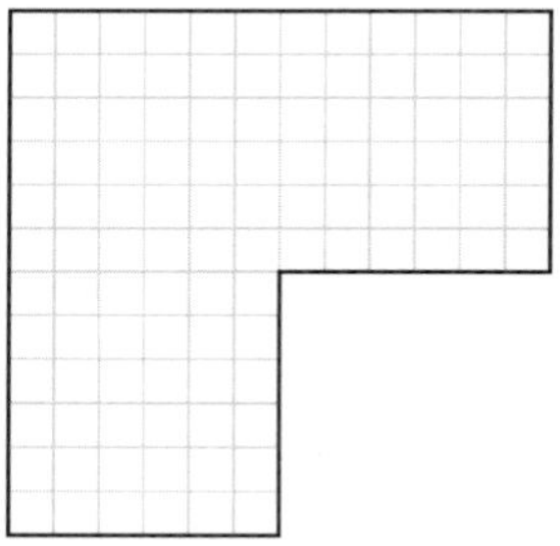

Answer : _____

㉑ Describe as many similar triangles as you can in the map of Midtown Manhattan in New York City.

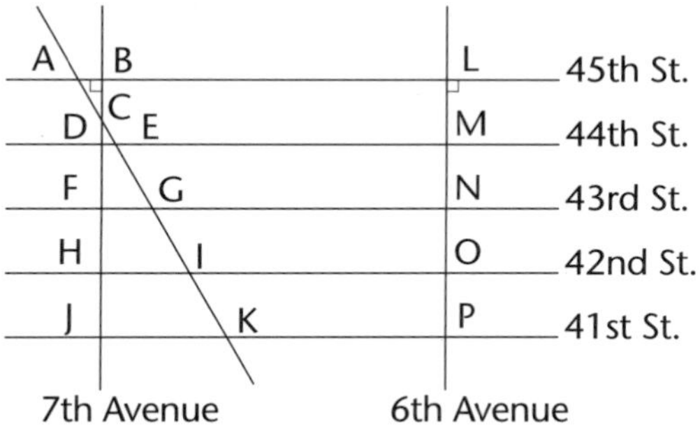

Answer : _____

㉒ The figure is called a tetrahedron.

   a.   What is the shape of each face?

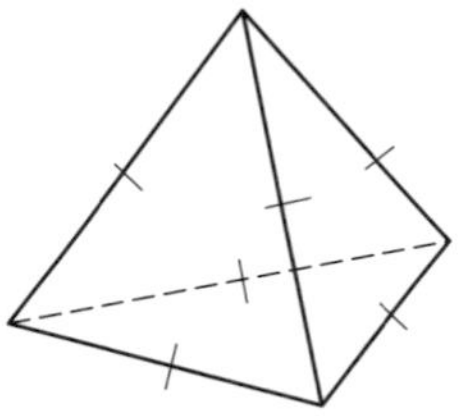

Answer : _____

   b.   Are all the faces congruent?

Answer : _____

CHALLENGE

① Divide the rectangle into 2 smaller rectangles by drawing a line parallel to the shorter side. Where should you draw the line so that the 2 smaller rectangles are similar but not congruent?

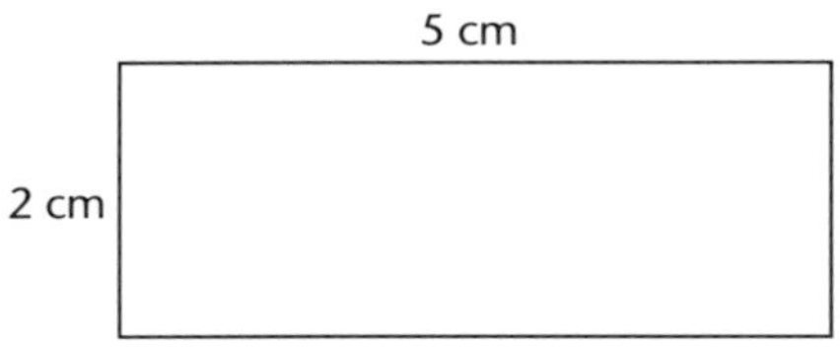

② How many squares can you construct by joining the dots on this 5 x 5 grid? How many are similar? How many are congruent groups?

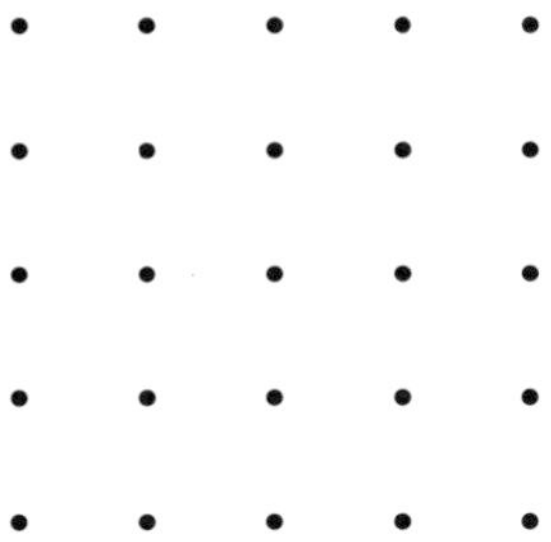

Answer : _____

EXAMPLE

a. Draw the translation, reflection and rotation images of the following marked squares.

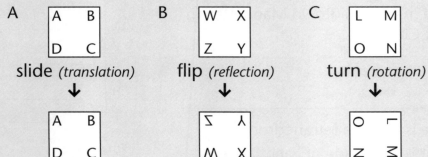

b. Which figure has line symmetry and which has rotational symmetry? Explain.

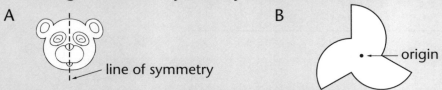

Answer : Figure A has line symmetry as there is only a reflection image. Figure B has rotational symmetry as it fits onto itself in less than one full turn.

Solve the problems. Show your work.

① Which of the diagrams below illustrate a translation?

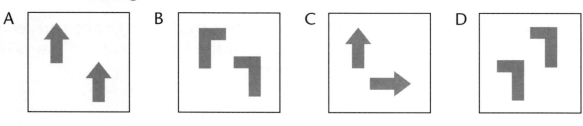

Answer : _____

② Which of the diagrams below illustrate a reflection?

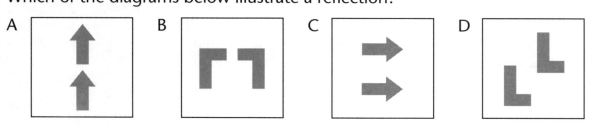

Answer : _____

③   Which of the diagrams below illustrate a rotation?

A      B   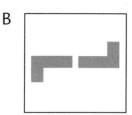   C   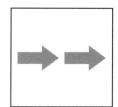   D 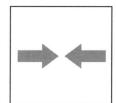

Answer : _____

④   Look how Bill moves a piece of glass with a letter B and a dot on it. Write the transformations.

a.   → → →

b.    → →

c.   →

Answer :   a.   b.   c.

⑤   You are helping Bill create an imaginative design for his paved driveway. Use a transformation of your choice to create the pattern. Draw at least 6 additional triangles on the grid below. Describe the transformation used.

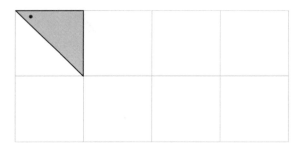

Answer : _____

⑥   The pattern on the wall paper in Bill's bedroom is made up of congruent rectangles. Describe the transformation associated with the arrangement.

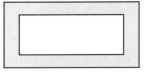 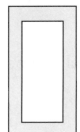 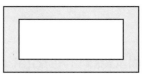 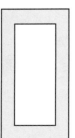

Answer : _____

⑦ A traditional Canadian quilt contains the following 7 shapes.

A   B   C   D   E   F   G

a.   Match them up in pairs, one being a rotation of the other.

Answer : _____

b.   Which shape does not have a match? Create a rotational image of that shape.

Answer : _____

⑧ Determine the number of lines of symmetry in each of the following flags.

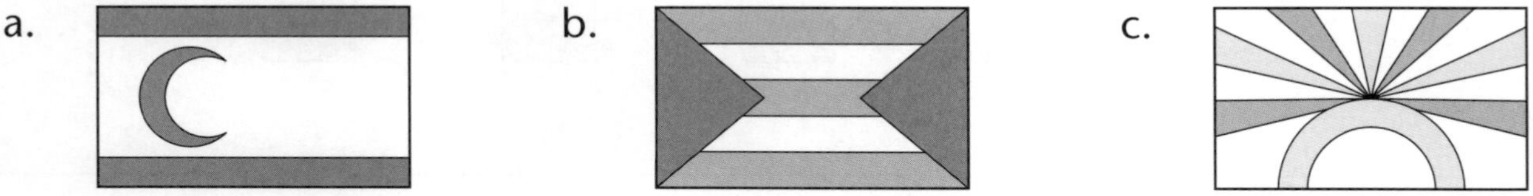

a.   b.   c.

Answer : a.   b.   c.

⑨ The following shapes are found in Mrs White's Math classroom.

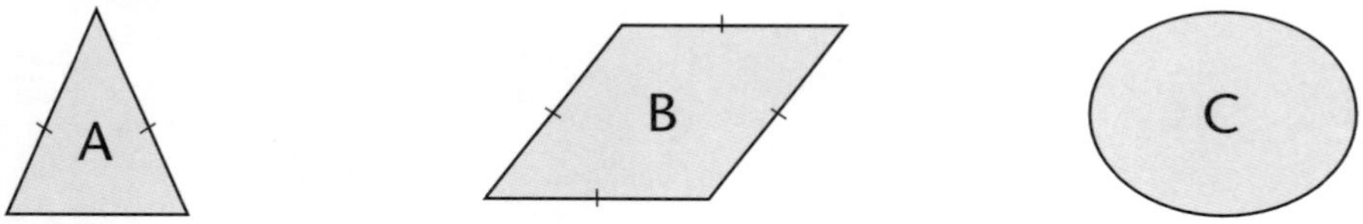

A   B   C

a.   Determine if each has rotational symmetry.

Answer : _____

b.   If a shape has rotational symmetry, state all clockwise fractional turns that rotate the object onto itself.

Answer : _____

⑩ Do these propeller blades have rotational symmetry or line symmetry?

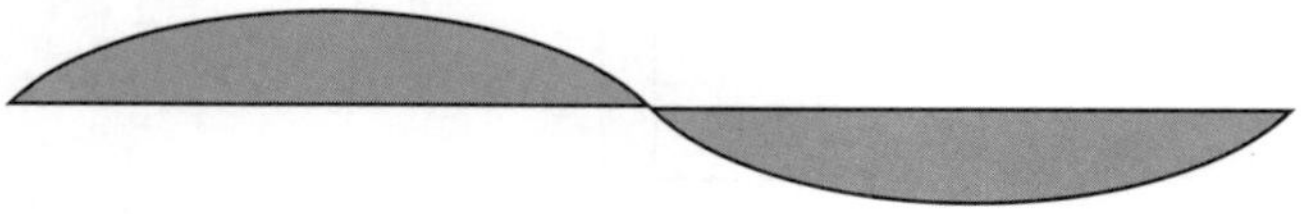

Answer : _____

⑪ The figure below has rotational symmetry. What is the order of the symmetry?

• A pattern which fits on itself in less than a complete rotation has rotational symmetry. If it fits on itself 3 times before it returns to its original position, it has rotational symmetry of order 4.

Read this first.

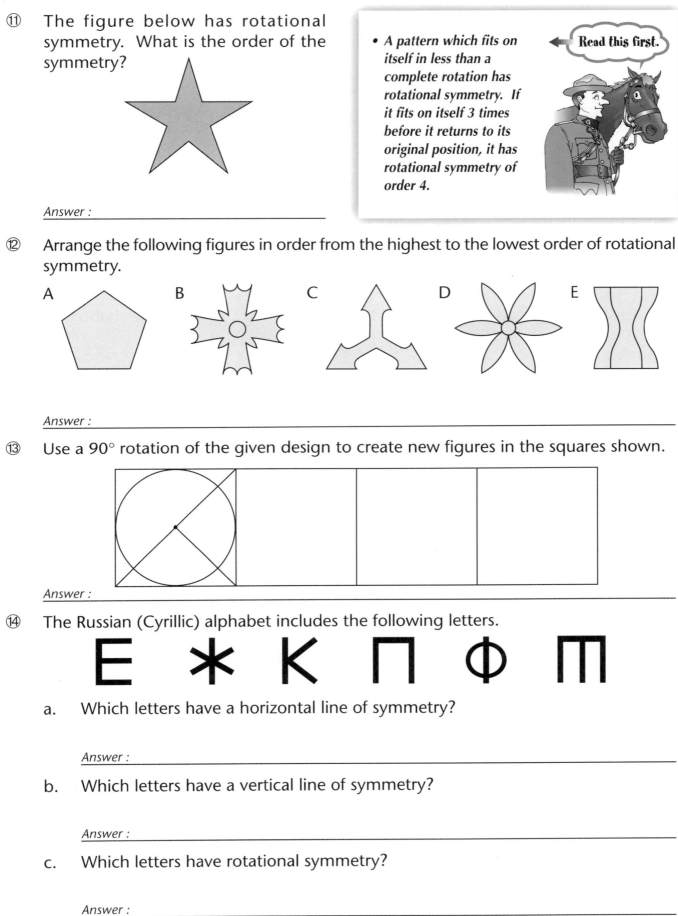

Answer : _____

⑫ Arrange the following figures in order from the highest to the lowest order of rotational symmetry.

A   B   C   D   E

Answer : _____

⑬ Use a 90° rotation of the given design to create new figures in the squares shown.

Answer : _____

⑭ The Russian (Cyrillic) alphabet includes the following letters.

Е Ж К П Ф Ш

a.   Which letters have a horizontal line of symmetry?

Answer : _____

b.   Which letters have a vertical line of symmetry?

Answer : _____

c.   Which letters have rotational symmetry?

Answer : _____

⑮ M.C. Escher made many pictures with different figures. Which of them can cover a flat surface without gaps or overlaps?

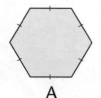 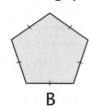 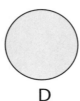 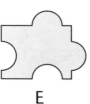 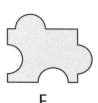

A   B   C   D   E   F

Answer : _____

⑯ Find at least 4 letters of the alphabet which can make a tiling pattern.

Answer : _____

⑰ Create a tiling pattern on the grid below with at least 10 of the tile shape shown.

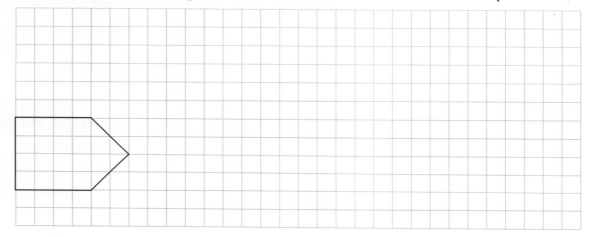

Answer : _____

Use the geoboard or dot paper to answer each of the following questions.

⑱ Draw the images of triangle A on the geoboard

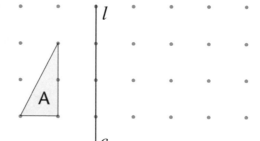

a. translated 5 right and 3 down (label the triangle B).

b. rotated 180° about the point *c* (label the triangle C).

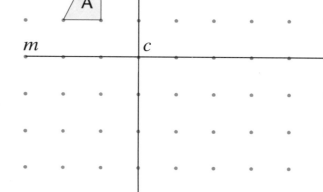

c. reflected in the line *l* (label the triangle D).

d. reflected in the line *m* (label the triangle E).

⑲ Peter has drawn 4 parallelograms on the dot paper as shown.

a. Compare the areas of the parallelograms.

Answer : _____

b. Describe the transformations which transfer K to L, K to M, and K to N.

Answer : _____

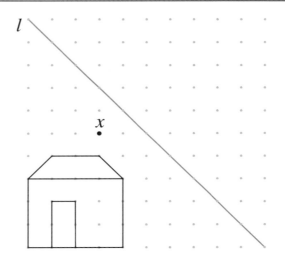

⑳ Ann has drawn a house on the dot paper. Draw the images of the house

a. rotated 180° about the point x (label the house B).

b. reflected in the line l (label the house C).

c. translated 6 right and 1 up (label the house D).

CHALLENGE

① Can a figure have line symmetry but not rotational symmetry? Explain with an example of a figure.

Answer : _____

② Draw a figure which has rotational symmetry of order 3 but does not have line symmetry.

Answer : _____

Solve the problems. Show your work.

①   Bill decides to build a scale model of the family cottage for his Technology project. The scale of the model is 1:100. The family cottage looks like a rectangular prism and its dimensions are 12 m by 12 m by 3 m.

     a.   Determine the dimensions of the model.

Answer : _____

     b.   How much space is there inside the model?

Answer : _____

     c.   How much cardboard is needed to make the model? Do not consider the window and the door.

Answer : _____

     d.   How many times is the space occupied by the cottage bigger than that occupied by the model?

Answer : _____

     e.   How many times is the interior surface area of the cottage bigger than that of the model?

Answer : _____

     f.   Which of the following nets can Bill use to construct his model? Circle the right answer.

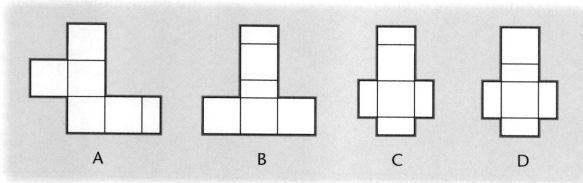

A   B   C   D

② Peter has made a model of a barn with cardboard and 27 2-cm cubes. Look at his model and solve the problems.

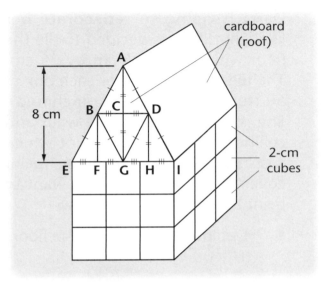

a. How many triangles are similar to △ABC?

Answer : _____

b. How many triangles are congruent to △ABD?

Answer : _____

c. Find the area of the parallelogram BDGE.

Answer : _____

d. Find the area of the trapezoid BDIE.

Answer : _____

e. If AI is 8.5 cm, what is the total surface area of the roof?

Answer : _____

f. What is the total surface area of the model?

Answer : _____

g. If Peter removes the part made with cardboard and paints the outside of the 6-cm cube, how many of the 2-cm cubes will have 2 painted faces?

Answer : _____

h. Peter submerged the 6-cm cube into the water in a rectangular container as shown. What was the original height of the water?

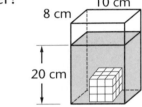

Answer : _____

i. Peter has 9 identical stickers. He has put one of them on a surface of the 6-cm cube. Help him put all the stickers onto the surface so that they are the reflection images of the sticker at the centre.

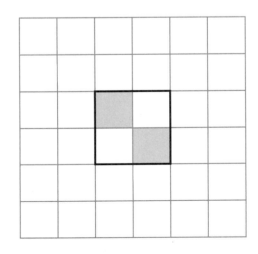

③ Dana is going to redecorate her kitchen. She has decided to tile the floor with tiles of 25 cm by 25 cm. The tiles cost $21.95 for each box of 50 (full boxes must be purchased). She is going to paint the walls and ceiling with 2 coats of paint which costs $27.99 / 4 L. Each litre of paint covers 4 m². She does not want to paint the door or the window.

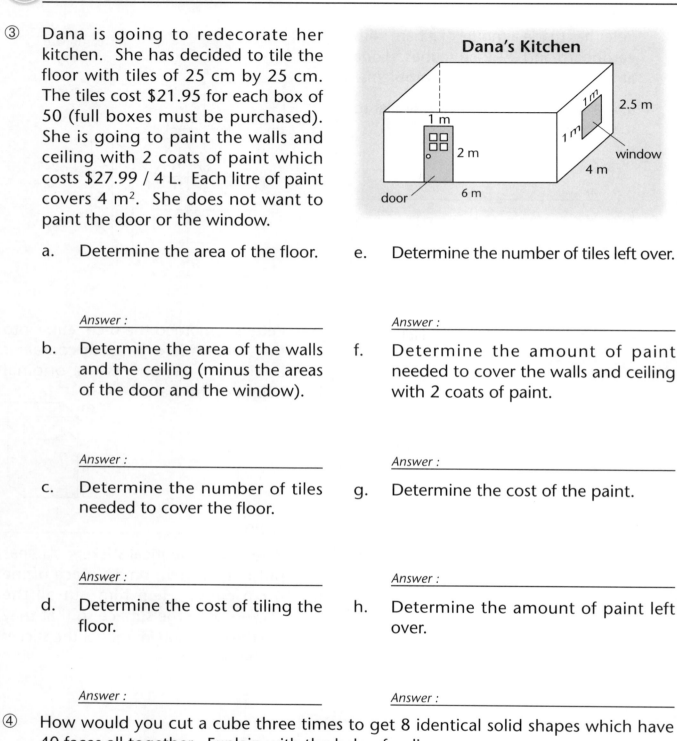

Dana's Kitchen

a. Determine the area of the floor.

Answer : _____

e. Determine the number of tiles left over.

Answer : _____

b. Determine the area of the walls and the ceiling (minus the areas of the door and the window).

Answer : _____

f. Determine the amount of paint needed to cover the walls and ceiling with 2 coats of paint.

Answer : _____

c. Determine the number of tiles needed to cover the floor.

Answer : _____

g. Determine the cost of the paint.

Answer : _____

d. Determine the cost of tiling the floor.

Answer : _____

h. Determine the amount of paint left over.

Answer : _____

④ How would you cut a cube three times to get 8 identical solid shapes which have 40 faces all together. Explain with the help of a diagram.

Answer : _____

⑤ David drew 2 similar triangles as shown. Determine the perimeter of △XYZ.

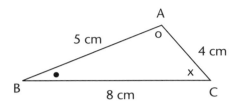 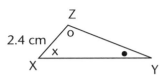

Answer : _____

⑥ You are going to tile the floor of your kitchen. Which of the following tiles would you not consider? Explain.

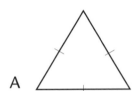 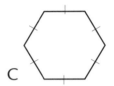 

Answer : _____

⑦ Mrs Chan has many interlocking bricks which are regular octagons. She cannot make a tiling pattern with the bricks when she uses them to pave her driveway. What should she do? Draw the pattern.

Answer : _____

⑧ For each of the following diagrams, draw all the lines of symmetry. Then determine the order of rotational symmetry.

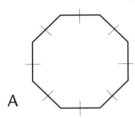  

A   B   C

Answer : A: _____ lines of symmetry. Rotational symmetry of order _____ .

B: _____ lines of symmetry. Rotational symmetry of order _____ .

C: _____ lines of symmetry. Rotational symmetry of order _____ .

UNIT 5 Data Management

EXAMPLE

28 Grade 7 students recorded their weights in kg as follows:

42, 35, 37, 41, 45, 39, 40, 49, 48, 51, 40, 38, 36, 39,

45, 48, 40, 40, 50, 41, 42, 40, 39, 44, 47, 48, 50, 40

Make a tally chart to organize the data and graph the weights using a circle graph.

a. **Tally chart / Frequency table**

Weight (kg)	Tally	Frequency (No. of students)
30 – 39	ℋℋ //	7
40 – 49	ℋℋ ℋℋ ℋℋ ///	18
50 – 59	///	3

b.

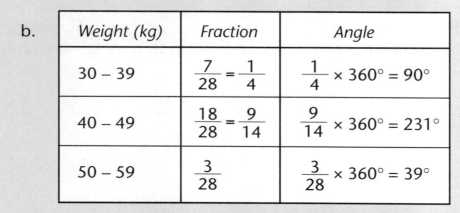

Weight (kg)	Fraction	Angle
30 – 39	$\frac{7}{28} = \frac{1}{4}$	$\frac{1}{4} \times 360° = 90°$
40 – 49	$\frac{18}{28} = \frac{9}{14}$	$\frac{9}{14} \times 360° = 231°$
50 – 59	$\frac{3}{28}$	$\frac{3}{28} \times 360° = 39°$

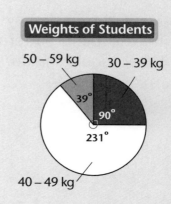

Weights of Students

50 – 59 kg   30 – 39 kg

39°

90°

231°

40 – 49 kg

Circle the correct answer in each problem.

① What type of graph would you draw to represent each of the following?

a. Toronto's maximum temperature each day for a week.

     A. pictograph   B. line graph   C. bar graph   D. circle graph

b. The scores of all football teams in the World Cup.

     A. line graph   B. circle graph   C. pictograph   D. bar graph

c. The percentage of your weekly expenditure on different activities.

     A. circle graph   B. pictograph   C. bar graph   D. line graph

28   *MathSmart : Problem-Solving (7B)*

② The circle graphs below show the fraction of Canada's population under 19 years old in the years 1900 and 1990. Which conclusion can you draw from the graphs?

A. The total population in Canada remained unchanged from 1900 to 1990.

B. The number of people under 19 years old decreased from 1900 to 1990.

C. The percentage of population under 19 years old decreased from 1900 to 1990.

D. There are more males than females under 19 years old.

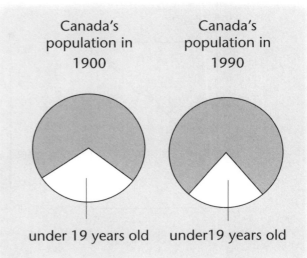

Canada's population in 1900   Canada's population in 1990

under 19 years old   under19 years old

Use the graphs to answer the questions.

③ The graph shows the percentage of female workers in a factory from 1990 to 2000.

a. When was there the greatest increase in the percentage of female workers?

Answer : _____

b. When was there a decrease in the percentage of female workers?

Answer : _____

Percentage of Female Workers

Female workers (in %)

35
30
25
20
15
10
5
0
1990 1992 1994 1996 1998 2000 2002
Year

c. Could a circle graph be used to represent the given data? Explain.

d. If the current trend continues, what percentage of female workers would be expected in the year 2002?

Answer : _____

Answer : _____

④ Explain what is wrong with each of the following graphs and what message each graph is meant to convey.

A. Sales of Ruby Red Wine in Ontario

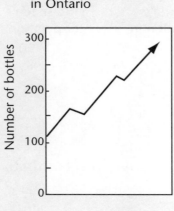

B. Absenteeism in November

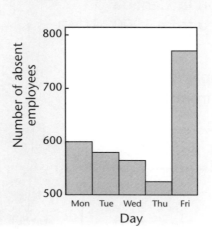

C. Prices of 1 Litre of Gas in Ontario

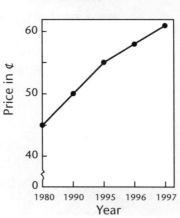

Answer : Graph A : _____

_____

Answer : Graph B : _____

_____

Answer : Graph C : _____

_____

⑤ The graphs below show the profits earned by a certain drug company between 1990 and 1999 in millions of dollars.

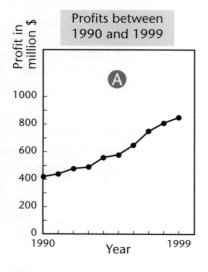

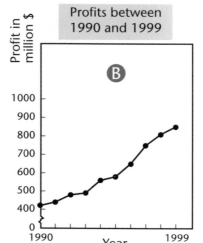

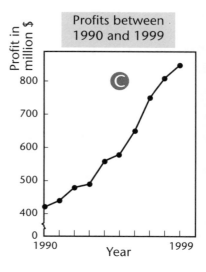

a. Which of these graphs would you use if you were

    i.   the President of the company at a meeting of shareholders? Explain.

        Answer : _____

    ii.   a politician talking about excessive drug company profits? Explain.

        Answer : _____

    iii. the President of the company explaining to the press that drug company profits are not excessive?

        Answer : _____

b. Predict what the company profit might be in the year 2000.

    Answer : _____

c. Use the data below to draw a bar graph showing the profits made by the company between 1990 and 1999.

Year	Profit (in million $)
1990	420
1991	450
1992	490
1993	500
1994	530
1995	570
1996	620
1997	730
1998	800
1999	850

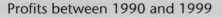

Profits between 1990 and 1999

⑥ 60 students were asked which form of exercise they preferred. The results are given in the chart below.

a. Complete the chart.

Activity	Number of students	Angle in a circle
Cycling	10	
Running	15	
Swimming	25	
Aerobics	10	

b. Draw a circle graph to illustrate the results.

c. What other type of graph could be used in this case?

Answer : _____

d. What type of graph would not be suitable?

Answer : _____

⑦ The following scores were recorded for a recent Math test.

58, 68, 72, 95, 37, 50, 75, 66, 83, 89, 48, 52, 64, 67, 75, 79, 85, 91

a. Organize the data into a stem-and-leaf plot.

b. Organize the data into a frequency table.

c. Graph the data using a bar graph.

d. Graph the data using a circle graph.

e. What percentage of students passed the test if the passing mark was 50?

Answer : _____

CHALLENGE

The graph shows the variation in the price of 1 oz of gold in US dollars in 1999.

① When did gold reach its highest value and lowest value?

Price (US$)

Price of 1 oz of gold

350

300

250

0
J F M A M J J A S O N D
Month

Answer : _____

② What was the percentage change in the value of gold between January 1 and December 31, 1999?

Answer : _____

③ What was the percentage change from the lowest to the highest value?

Answer : _____

Analysis of Data

EXAMPLE

15 students recorded their heights in centimetres as follows:

150, 147, 155, 154, 160, 158, 148, 156, 155, 162, 170, 165, 163, 145, 153

Make a stem-and-leaf plot and use it to calculate the 3 measures of central tendency — mean (average), median (middle value) and mode (most common value).

Solutions :

tens	ones
14	5, 7, 8
15	0, 3, 4, 5, 5, 6, 8
16	0, 2, 3, 5
17	0

mean : $\dfrac{\text{sum of values}}{\text{number of values}}$

$= \dfrac{2341}{15}$

$= 156$

median : middle value
= 8th value (7 values below and 7 above)
= 155

mode : most common value
= 155 (occurs twice)

Solve the problems. Show your work.

① For each of the following statements, create a set of data with at least 3 values which will make the statement true.

a. The mean is smaller than the mode.

Answer : _____

b. The mode is smaller than the mean.

Answer : _____

c. The median is smaller than the mean.

Answer : _____

d. The mean is smaller than the median.

Answer : _____

e. The mode and the median are the same.

Answer : _____

f. The mean of the values is 7.

Answer : _____

② The Toronto Hockey Team had the following number of shots on goal last month:

15, 20, 20, 15, 18, 23, 18, 24, 18

- If there is an even number of values, the _median_ is the average of the 2 middle values.
- There may be more than 1 _mode_ or none at all.

Read this first.

a.   Determine the mean.

Answer : _____

b.   Arrange the numbers in order and determine the median and the mode.

Answer : _____

c.   If one additional game was played, with 29 shots on goal, would this affect the mean, median and/or mode? Explain.

Answer : The mean _____

_____ The median _____

_____ The mode _____

③ The stem-and-leaf diagram below shows the number of hours of TV viewing per week by a group of 13-year-olds in Toronto.

tens	ones	tens	ones
0	7, 9	3	5, 5, 5, 8, 8
1	1, 2, 4, 4, 8, 8, 9	4	2, 2
2	1, 3, 4, 6, 6, 8, 8		

a.   Use the diagram to determine the mean of the number of hours of TV viewing per week. (correct to 2 decimal places)

Answer : _____

b.   Determine the median and the mode.

Answer : _____

④ The table below shows the annual salaries of the employees of ABC Construction Company.

Annual salary per person	Number of employees
$30 000.00	12
$40 000.00	2
$45 000.00	3
$60 000.00	2
$100 000.00	1 (President)

a. Calculate the mean, median and mode of the annual salaries.

Answer : _____

b. In an advertisement to attract new employees for the company, would you use the mean, median or mode? Why?

Answer : _____

c. If the President got a pay increase, would this affect the mean, median or mode?

Answer : _____

d. Which measure of central tendency best represents the given salaries? Why?

Answer : _____

⑤ The regular price of an ice cream cone is $1.25 but on Mondays it sells for $0.95. Karen and her friends bought 5 ice cream cones on Saturday, 3 on Sunday and 4 on Monday. Calculate the average price they paid.

Answer : _____

⑥ Dan and his classmates are talking about their weekly allowances for lunch. Dan has $25.00, 2 of his classmates have $32.00 each, 3 have $24.00 each, and 4 have $28.00 each. Jane brings sandwiches to school for lunch and has no allowance. Determine the mean of the allowances of the children. (correct to 2 decimal places)

Answer : _____

⑦ Determine the mean, median and range of the following set of test results.

68, 70, 72, 78, 78

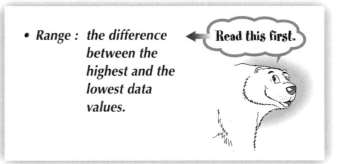

• Range : the difference between the highest and the lowest data values.

Read this first.

Answer : _____

⑧ The line graph shows the winning heights in Women's High Jump at the Olympic Games between 1968 and 1996. Use the graph to answer the following questions.

a. What trend do you notice in the winning heights?

Answer : _____

b. Calculate the approximate average winning height over the interval shown on the graph.

Answer : _____

c. Predict what the winning height might be in 2000.

Answer : _____

Winning Heights in Women's High Jump

Height (m)

d. What is the range of these data values?

Answer : _____

⑨ A class of 25 students averaged 70% on a test. Another class of 30 students averaged 60%. Calculate the average percentage of all the 55 students.

Answer : _____

⑩ The average of 3 numbers is 20. One of the numbers is 15. Calculate the sum of the other 2 numbers.

Answer : _____

⑪ The table shows the number of oil tanker spills worldwide between 1982 and 1990.

Year	1982	1983	1984	1985	1986	1987	1988	1989	1990
Number of spills	9	17	15	9	8	12	13	31	8

a. Determine the mean, median and mode(s).

Answer : The mean _____ ; the median _____ ; the mode(s) _____ .

b. Which best reflects the data, the mode(s) or mean? Explain your answer.

Answer : _____

c. If you were a member of an environmental organization, which measure would you use? Why?

Answer : _____

d. If you were the president of an oil company, which measure would you use? Why?

Answer : _____

⑫ The annual sales of Evesview Company are shown on the bar graph.

a. Use the graph to determine the average (mean) sales of the company between 1991 and 1995.

Answer : _____

b. The graph shows a rapid increase in annual sales. How is this impression created?

Answer : _____

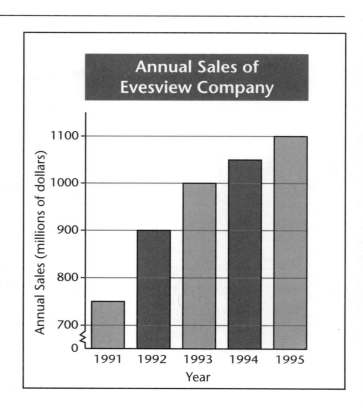

Annual Sales of Evesview Company

⑬ The table below shows the population density of some East Asian countries in 1992. Use the table to answer the questions.

a. Calculate the population density of each country to complete the table.

Country	Area (thousands of sq. km)	Population (millions)	Population Density ($\frac{Population}{Area}$)
Indonesia	1882	197	
Japan	374	125	
Philippines	297	67	
North Korea	120	22	
South Korea	97	44	

b. Which of these countries is the most densely populated?

Answer : _____

c. Determine the mean population size of these countries (in millions).

Answer : _____

d. Determine the median population size of these countries (in millions).

Answer : _____

e. Which type of graph could be used to represent these statistics? (Do not draw the graph.)

Answer : _____

CHALLENGE

7 students' test scores are recorded with a mean of 55%, a median of 60% and a mode of 70%. If the lowest score is 34% and the highest score is 71%, determine the 5 possible groups of test scores.

Answer : A. _____   D. _____

B. _____   E. _____

C. _____

MathSmart : Problem-Solving (7B)

39

EXAMPLE

Jimmie wants to buy a new bike. He can choose a mountain bike or an all-terrain bike. The colours available are black, silver, white and gold. If all choices are equally likely,

a.   in how many ways can Jimmie choose a new bike?

b.   what is the probability that his bike will be black?

c.   what is the probability that it will be an all-terrain bike?

d.   what is the probability that it will be a black all-terrain bike?

Solutions :

Tree Diagram

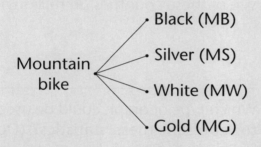

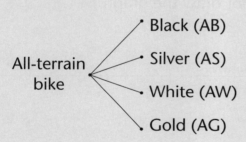

a.   Jimmie can choose a bike in 8 ways.

b.   P(black) = $\dfrac{\text{No. of bikes which are black}}{\text{Total number of bikes}}$

$= \dfrac{2}{8} = \dfrac{1}{4}$

c.   P(all-terrain) = $\dfrac{\text{No. of all-terrain bikes}}{\text{Total number of bikes}}$

$= \dfrac{4}{8} = \dfrac{1}{2}$

d.   P(black all-terrain) :

$= \dfrac{\text{No. of black all-terrain bikes}}{\text{Total number of bikes}}$

$= \dfrac{1}{8}$

Solve the problems. Show your work.

①   Ann flipped a coin 50 times and heads turned up 24 times.

a.   What fraction of the flips turned up heads?

Answer : _____

b.   Is this what you would expect?

Answer : _____

c. If the coin is fair and Ann flips the coin 500 times, how many times should she expect it to come up heads?

Answer : _____

d. What fraction of the flips should come up heads if she flips the coin many times?

Answer : _____

e. If the first 5 flips are all heads, what is the probability that the next flip will be heads?

Answer : _____

f. Is it possible to flip a coin 20 times and have it turn up heads every time? Is this likely to happen?

Answer : _____

② Carol and Debbie play a coin-tossing game. They take turns tossing 2 coins. If both coins match, Carol gets a point. If the coins don't match, Debbie gets a point. The first player to get 10 points wins. Who is likely to win? Illustrate your answer with a tree diagram in the box.

Answer : _____

③ Eric and Frank also play a coin-tossing game but they use 3 coins. If 3 coins match, Eric gets a point. If only 2 coins match, Frank gets a point. The first to score 10 points wins. Who is likely to win? Illustrate your answer with a tree diagram in the box.

Answer : _____

④ George spun each of the spinners below 30 times.

 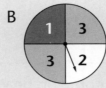 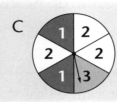

a. What is the probability that the result will be a 3 in each case?

Answer : _____

b. How many times should he expect each spinner to land on a 3?

Answer : _____

c. Does the probability of landing on a 3 depends on the number of times he spun each spinner?

Answer : _____

d. Which of the spinners would give a fair game of chance?

Answer : _____

⑤ In a TV guessing game, a bucket is filled with an unknown number of coloured balls. Members of the audience are asked to guess and write down, one after the other, the colour of the ball that would be drawn. If the guess is correct, they win a prize.

a. Would it be better to write first or last? Explain.

Answer : _____

b. If the bucket contains 10 red, 20 white and 30 black balls, what is the probability that a white ball will be drawn?

Answer : _____

c. What is the most likely outcome if the ball is drawn randomly?

Answer : _____

⑥ When I toss a fair die,

a. what is the probability that the die will show a 4?

b. what is the probability that the die will show a number greater than 4?

Answer : _____

Answer : _____

⑦ Mrs Smith has made 2 spinners to help determine what she will make for lunch.

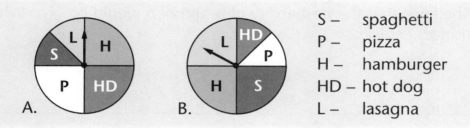

S – spaghetti
P – pizza
H – hamburger
HD – hot dog
L – lasagna

a. What is the probability that there will be hamburgers for lunch if only spinner B is spun?

Answer : _____

b. If you like spaghetti, which spinner would you like Mrs Smith to use?

c. Frankie uses spinner A to predict the outcome and gets points if his prediction is correct. He can get 2 points for guessing that the outcome is hamburger. How many points should he get for guessing lasagna? Explain.

Answer : _____

Answer : _____

⑧ When 2 dice are rolled and the numbers on the upper faces are added, there are 12 different possible sums.

a. Complete the sum chart below to show the possible outcomes.

⊕	1	2	3	4	5	6
1						
2						
3						
4						
5						
6						

b. Are all the different sums equally likely?

Answer : _____

c. What is the probability that the sum on the 2 dice is 4?

Answer : _____

d. Which sum is most likely?

Answer : _____

⑨ In Monopoly, you get out of jail if you roll a double with 2 dice. What is the probability that you roll a double?

Answer : _____

⑩ Trish has 5 different polyhedral dice. They have 4, 6, 8, 12 and 20 faces respectively. She rolls any 2 dice together and records the sums of the faces that come up.

a. She finds that the probability of a sum of 6 would be $\frac{5}{48}$. Which 2 dice is she using? Explain.

Answer : _____

b. Using the 2 dice you found in a, determine the probability of getting a sum of 13.

Answer : _____

⑪ On your next family vacation to Quebec, you plan to visit Quebec city, Montreal and Hull.

a. In how many different orders can you visit the 3 cities?

Answer : _____

b. In practice, would all orders be equally likely? Explain.

Answer : _____

⑫ Sylvia rolls 3 dice.

a. What is the probability that all 3 dice show a 6?

Answer : _____

b. What is the probability that all 3 dice show 4 or 5?

Answer : _____

c.   What is the probability that all dice match?

Answer : _____

⑬   A betting game consists of rolling a die. You only win if you roll a 6 and the prize is
$2. How much money do you expect to win by rolling the die 60 times?

Answer : _____

⑭   5 cards marked 1, 2, 3, 4 and 5 are in a bag. If 2 cards are taken from the bag, what
is the probability that

a.   both of them are even?

Answer : _____

b.   one of them is even?

Answer : _____

⑮   A scratch and match card is made with 4 scratch-off spots. 2 of the spots have the
same letter and the other 2 have different letters. To win, you must scratch only 2
spots and they must have the same letter.
What is the probability that you will win?

Answer : _____

𝒞𝐻𝐀𝐋𝐋𝐄𝐍𝒢𝐄

A CD club offers 4 monthly choices. You can choose any 2 CDs at a special discount
price. In how many different ways can you choose 2 CDs?

Answer : _____

Circle the correct answer in each problem.

① The perimeter of the larger square is 20 cm and the perimeter of the smaller square is 16 cm. What is the area of the region between the 2 squares?

A. 1 cm^2 B. 2 cm^2

C. 4 cm^2 D. 9 cm^2

② In a club of 24 members, each serves on three 4-person committees. How many committees are there?

A. 24   B. 32

C. 18   D. 12

③ The average of 3 numbers is between 7 and 10. The sum of the numbers could be any of the following EXCEPT

A. 22.   B. 20.

C. 28.   D. 26.

④ If each side of a square is increased by 50%, then the area of the square is increased by

A. 50%.   B. 100%.

C. 125%.   D. 225%.

⑤ You are joining a book club. You get 2 free choices from 4 books. How many different choices do you have?

A. 24   B. 8

C. 6   D. 12

⑥ The average (mean) of the first 10 positive whole numbers is

A. 5.   B. 5.5.

C. 6.   D. 10.

⑦ If 14 pigs equal 35 hogs, then 50 hogs equal

A. 125 pigs.   B. 70 pigs.

C. 20 pigs.   D. 7 pigs.

⑧ Jack takes 3 pairs of jeans, 4 T-shirts and 2 pairs of shoes for his trip. How many different outfits could he wear?

A. 9   B. 24

C. 12   D. 22

⑨ Ann, Bill, Carol and Dave serve on a school committee. In how many different ways could a President and Vice-President be chosen from the committee members?

A. 12   B. 6

C. 7   D. 8

⑩ How many squares are there in the following figure?

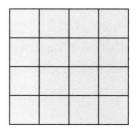

A. 16   B. 20

C. 25   D. 30

The table below shows Julie's Math test scores so far. Use the table to solve the problems. Show your work.

Test	1st	2nd	3rd	4th	5th	6th
Score (%)	85	82	91	72	75	85

⑪ Julie's teacher lets Julie choose the mean, median or mode of the scores to be recorded on her interim report card. Which one should Julie choose? Explain.

Answer : _____

⑫ There are 3 more tests to write this semester. How can Julie get a median of 85 for her 9 tests?

Answer : _____

⑬ How can she get a mean of 80 for her 9 tests?

Answer : _____

⑭ What type of graph could be used to represent Julie's test scores? Explain.

Answer : _____

⑮ If Julie's teacher picks a percentage at random from the 6 tests written so far, what is the probability that the grade will be a B (70 - 79%)?

Answer : _____

⑯ Mary is Julie's classmate. She got 83 on the 2nd Math test. What is her performance on the other 5 tests if she has the same median as Julie for her first 6 tests?

Answer : _____

⑰ What is Mary's performance if she has the same mode as Julie on her first 6 Math tests?

Answer : _____

⑱ Read the circle graph showing the time spent per day by a 12-year-old child on various activities.

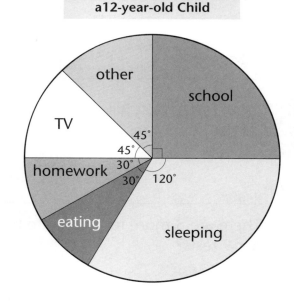

Time Spent Per Day by a12-year-old Child

a. According to the graph, how much time does a typical 12-year-old child spend on homework per day?

Answer : _____

b. What percentage of a day is spent on sleeping? (correct to the nearest 0.1%)

Answer : _____

c. Why is a circle graph the most suitable for this application?

Answer : _____

d. How might the circle graph differ for an 18-year-old teenager?

Answer : _____

Solve the problems. Show your work.

⑲ Briana is the marketing manager of a chocolate company. In order to promote a new brand of chocolate bar, she is planning a prize system whereby every 50th chocolate bar will contain a 50¢ off coupon and every 200th chocolate bar will contain a $2.00 discount coupon. No chocolate bars can contain 2 prizes.

a. Explain how she should distribute the prizes fairly in 500 boxes of chocolate bars, each box containing 20 bars.

Answer : _____

b. If Jim buys 10 chocolate bars, what is the probability that he will win something?

Answer : _____

c. If all the chocolate bars are sold and 80% of the prizes are claimed, how much will this promotion cost the company?

Answer : _____

⑳ The Richmond School Athletic Council held a casino night to raise money for school sports.

a. At the first table, the game consisted of spinning 3 spinners. Each spinner had a red, black, white and yellow sector. Jane tested each of the spinners by spinning 100 times and recorded the results on a graph. Use the graphs to help you decide what each of the spinners looked like. Explain your answers.

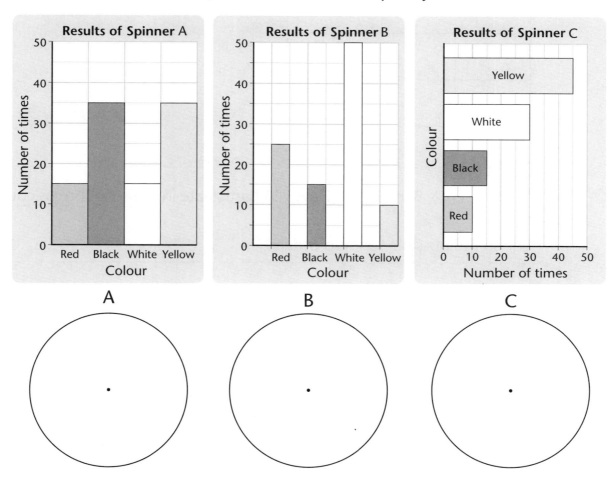

Answer : _____

b. At another table, the game consisted of tossing 2 coins. You only win if you can toss 2 heads. Brian tossed the pair of coins 20 times. How many times should he expect to win?

Answer : _____

㉑ 25 Grade 7 students recorded their ages in months as follows:

150   140   145   153   141   144   146   139   156   158   150   144   142
140   148   149   159   150   151   150   138   140   135   139   138

a. Make a stem-and-leaf plot and use it to determine the median age of the Grade 7 students.

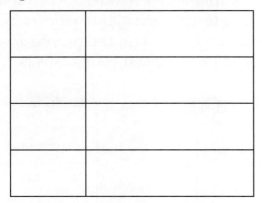

Answer : _____

b. Draw a suitable graph to show the ages of the Grade 7 students.

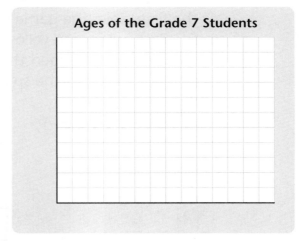

Answer : _____

㉒ Jim (J), Charles (C), Ben (B) and Dave (D) participate in the school cross country relay team.

a. List all the possible running orders.

b. How many different running orders are there?

Answer : _____

c. What is the probability that Jim will run first?

Answer : _____

d. If Charles is the fastest runner and should therefore run the last leg, how many different running orders are there?

Answer : _____

ANSWERS 7B

Unit 1

1. Area : (3 x 1.4 – 1.4 x 1.4) ÷ 2 = 2.24 ÷ 2 = 1.12
   The area is 1.12 m^2.
2. Area : 50 x 4 x 50 x 2 = 20000   The area is 20 000 cm^2.
3. The perimeter of the base : (60 + 36) x 2 = 192
   No of times : 3 x 1000 ÷ 192 = 15.625
   They must walk around 16 times.
4. a. Possible dimensions : 16 = 1 x 16; 2 x 8; 4 x 4
      Possible perimeters : (1 + 16) x 2 ; (2 + 8) x 2; (4 + 4) x 2
      The possible lengths are 34 m, 20 m and 16 m.
   b. The minimum length of fence is 16 m.
5. a. Sum of width and length : 20 ÷ 2 = 10
      Possible widths and lengths : (5,5); (6,4); (7,3); (8,2); (9,1)
      Possible areas : (5 x 5); (6 x 4); (7 x 3); (8 x 2); (9 x 1)
      The possible values for the areas are 25 m^2, 24 m^2, 21 m^2, 16 m^2
      and 9 m^2.
   b. Difference : 25 – 9 = 16   The difference is 16 m^2.
   c. • Rectangles with the same perimeter may have different areas.
      • The greater the difference between the length and width of a
        rectangle, the smaller the area of the rectangle.
6. No. of tiles : 100 x 100 ÷ 1 x 1 = 10000   He needs 10 000 tiles.
7. Perimeter : 10 + (16 – 8) + 1 + 8 + (10 – 1 – 7) + 16 = 45
   Cost : 45 x 15 = 675   The fencing costs $675.00.
8. Area : (5 + 1 + 1) x (7 + 1 + 1) – 5 x 7 = 28   The area is 28 m^2.
9. Area of backyard : 1 x (16 – 8) + (10 – 1) x 16 = 8 + 144 = 152
   Area to be planted : 152 – (5 + 1 + 1) x (7 + 1 + 1) = 89
   Cost : 89 x 12 = 1068   The cost of the grass will be $1068.00.
10. Floor area : 4 x 5 = 20
    Cost : 20 x 70 = 1400   The carpet costs $1400.00.
11. Total area : (5 x 2.5) x 2 + (4 x 2.5) x 2 – 7 + 5 x 4 = 58
    Amount of paint needed : 58 ÷ 5 = 11.6
    Cost of paint : 11.6 x 8.99 = 104.28   The cost of the paint is $104.28.
12. Total area : 10 x 2 x 8 = 160   The total area is 160 cm^2.
13. Perimeter : 24 ÷ 3 x 4 = 32   The perimeter is 32 cm.
14. Average area : 9 x 4 ÷ 3 = 12   The average area is 12 cm^2.
15. a. Perimeter : 12 + 12 + 6 = 30   The perimeter is 30 cm.
    b. Area : 6 x 11.62 ÷ 2 = 34.86   The area is 34.86 cm^2.
16. a. Perimeter : 50 x 6 = 300   The perimeter is 300 cm.
    b. Area : 88 x 24 ÷ 2 x 2 + 50 x 88 = 6512   The area is 6512 cm^2.
17. Shaded area : 2 x 3 ÷ 2 = 3   The area is 3 cm^2.
18. Area of square = area of triangle : 5 x 5 = 25
    Height of triangle : 25 x 2 ÷ 10 = 5   The height of the triangle is 5 cm.
19. Area : 3 x 4 ÷ 2 + 12 x 5 ÷ 2 = 6 + 30 = 36
    Perimeter : 4 + 3 + 13 + 12 = 32
    The area is 36 cm^2 and the perimeter is 32 cm.
20. Area : 6 x 5 + 6 x 3 ÷ 2 = 39   The area is 39 m^2.
21. Total area : (30 + 36) x 30 ÷ 2 x 2 = 1980
    Their total area is 1980 cm^2.
22. Total area : (44 + 48) x 30 ÷ 2 x 2 = 2760
    Their total area is 2760 cm^2.
23. Total area : (5 + 10) x 6 ÷ 2 ÷ 12 x 3 = 11.25
    The total area is 11.25 cm^2.
24. Shaded area : (1.2 + 2) x 1 ÷ 2 x 2 = 3.2   The area is 3.2 cm^2.
25. Area : (0.5 + 0.7) x (1 – 0.7) ÷ 2 + 0.7 x 0.7 = 0.67
    Its cross-sectional area is 0.67 m^2.

Challenge

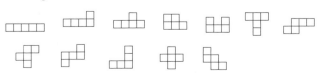

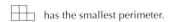 has the smallest perimeter.

Unit 2

1. 1m^3 = 100 cm x 100 cm x 100 cm = 1000000 cm^3
   There are 1 000 000 cm^3 in 1 m^3.
2. 1m^2 = 100 cm x 100 cm = 10000 cm^2
   There are 10000 cm^2 in 1 m^2.
3. Volume : 12 x 12 x 12 = 1728;   Capacity : 1728 ÷ 1000 = 1.728
   It can contain 1.728 L of water.
4. Area of each surface : 54 ÷ 6 = 9
   Length of each side : $\sqrt{9} = \sqrt{3 \times 3} = 3$
   The dimensions are 3 cm x 3 cm x 3 cm.
5.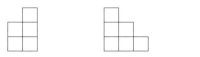
6. Before k is removed, there are 4 x 6 = 24 surfaces.
   After k is removed, there are still 24 surfaces.
   No effect. The total number of surfaces remains the same.
7. a. The total surface area will increase.
   b. 4 more surfaces will be exposed. Total area : 2 x 2 x 4 = 16
      There is an increase of 16 cm^2.
8. a. Dimensions : (12 ÷ 4) by (12 ÷ 4) by (12 – 3 x 2)
      The dimensions are 3 cm by 3 cm by 6 cm.
   b. Total surface area : 3 x 3 x 2 + 3 x 6 x 4 = 18 + 72 = 90
      The total surface area is 90 cm^2.
   c. Volume : 3 x 3 x 6 = 54   The volume is 54 cm^3.
9. Total surface area of the gift :
   20 x 30 x 2 + 8 x 30 x 2 + 20 x 8 x 2 = 2000
   Area of the paper : 100 x 100 = 10000 (10000 > 2000)
   She will have enough paper.
10. a. Assume each side of the cube is 1 cm.   Total surface area : 1 x 6 = 6
       Total surface area of a 2 cm cube : 2 x 2 x 6 = 24
       No. of times : 24 ÷ 6 = 4   The surface area has increased by 4 times.
    b. Volume : 1 x 1 x 1 = 1;   New volume : 2 x 2 x 2 = 8
       No. of times : 8 ÷ 1 = 8   The volume has increased by 8 times.
11. A cube has 6 faces. Surface area of each face : 216 ÷ 6 = 36
    Length of each side : $\sqrt{36}$ = 6;   Volume : 6 x 6 x 6 = 216
    The volume is 216 m^3.
12. a. Amount of wood : 1.5 x 1 x 2 + 1.2 x 1 x 2 + 1.5 x 1.2 x 2 = 9
       The amount of wood required is 9 m^2.
    b. Volume : 1.2 x 1.5 x 1 = 1.8   The volume is 1.8 m^3.
13. Total area to be painted : 5 x 4 x 1 + 4 x 3 x 2 + 5 x 3 x 2 – 3 = 71
    Number of cans needed : 71 x 2 ÷ 36 = 3.94
    I need 4 cans of 4 L paint.
14. No. of dice : (10 x 10 x 10) ÷ (2 x 2 x 2) = 125
    125 dice can be placed in the box.
15. Volume : 30 x 16 x 23 x 3 + 20 x 16 x 23 x 1.5 = 44160
    The minimum volume of the container is 44 160 cm^3.
16. Box A : 11.99 ÷ (17 x 30 x 30) = 0.00078
    Box B : 6.99 ÷ (15 x 25 x 25) = 0.00075 (0.00075 < 0.00078)
    Box B is a better buy.
17. No. of servings : (31 x 20 x 7) ÷ 175 = 24...140
    It contains 24 servings.
18. 27m^3/h for 1 workman; 54 m^3/h for 2 workmen.
    Time taken : (6 x 6 x 6) ÷ 54 = 4   They would take 4 hours.
19. Volume of the pyramid : 5 x 5 x 12 x $\frac{1}{3}$ = 100
    New water level : 12 + 100 ÷ (5 x 5) = 12 + 4 = 16
    The new water level will be 16 cm.
20. There are 15 rectangular prisms with (30 x 20 x 150)cm^3.
    Volume of cement needed : 30 x 20 x 150 x 15 = 1350000
    The volume of cement needed is 1 350 000 cm^3 (1.35m^3).
21. Length of each side of cardboard : $\sqrt{25}$ = 5
    Capacity of the open box : (5 – 2) x 1 x (5 – 2) = 9
    The capacity is 9 mL.

22. Volume of the tank : 3 x 1 x 1 – 1 x 0.5 x 1 = 2.5
    The volume of the tank is 2.5 m³ (2 500 000 cm³).
    Time needed : 2500000 ÷ (20 x 1000) = 125
    It would take 125 minutes (2 hr 5 min).
23. No. of cubes : 4 x 4 x 2 + 4 x 2 x 4 = 64
    64 cubes will have just one face painted.

Challenge
1.
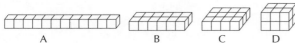
    A   B   C   D

2. A : 1 x 12 x 4 + 1 x 1 x 2 = 50
   B : 2 x 6 x 2 + 1 x 6 x 2 + 1 x 2 x 2 = 40
   C : 3 x 4 x 2 + 1 x 4 x 2 + 1 x 3 x 2 = 38
   D : 2 x 3 x 4 + 2 x 2 x 2 = 32
   The surface area of each prism is 50 cm², 40 cm², 38 cm², 32 cm².
3. Yes. The volume of each prism is 12 cm³.

Unit 3

1. False   2. True   3. False
4. True   5. True   6. True
7. The scale is 1:300; 15 m = 1500 cm; 18 m = 1800 cm.
   Dimensions on the blueprint : $\frac{1500}{300} = 5$; $\frac{1800}{300} = 6$
   The dimensions are 5 cm by 6 cm.
8. Ratio of the widths : $\frac{3.6}{3} = \frac{1.2}{1}$
   Ratio of the lengths : $\frac{8.4}{7} = \frac{1.2}{1}$
   Yes. They are similar to each other because corresponding sides are in the same ratio.
9. Ratio of the widths : $\frac{37}{26}$
   Ratio of the lengths : $\frac{27}{21} = \frac{9}{7}$ ($\frac{37}{26} \neq \frac{27}{21}$)
   No. They are not similar to each other because corresponding sides are not in the same ratio.
10. 540 m = 54000 cm
    54 000 is represented by 6 or 9000 is represented by 1.
    The scale is 1:9000.
11. Yes. Both triangles are equal in size and shape.
12. Length : $\frac{3}{2}$ x 1.2 = 1.8; $\frac{3}{1.2}$ x 2 = 5
    The length of the other 2 sides is either 1.8 cm or 5 cm.
13. 10.8:7.2 = X:5;   X = $\frac{10.8}{7.2}$ x 5 = 7.5   X is 7.5 cm long.
14. 5.4:7.2 = X:4.2;   X = 4.2 x $\frac{5.4}{7.2}$ = 3.15
    A = 120°(corresponding angles)   X is 3.15 cm long; angle A is 120°.
15. 9.6:20 = width:14;   width = $\frac{9.6}{20}$ x 14 = 6.72
    The width is 6.72 cm.
16. Ratio of the corresponding sides : $\frac{2.4}{3} = \frac{0.8}{1} = \frac{4}{5} = \frac{1.2}{1.5}$
    Yes. They are similar to each other because all sides are proportional.
17. Ratio of the corresponding sides : $\frac{9}{6} = \frac{6}{4}$
    Yes. They are similar to each other because corresponding sides are proportional.
18. No. The two triangles are not necessarily congruent since the sides may be different in length.
19. Yes. The equilateral triangles are similar since corresponding sides are in the same ratio.
20. The area of each shape is 27 square units.

21. △CBA, △CDE, △CFG, △CHI and △CJK are similar triangles.

22. a. Each face is an equilateral triangle.
    b. Yes. All the faces are congruent.

Challenge
1.
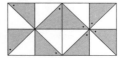

2.
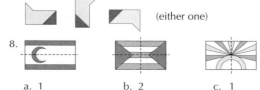

Dimensions	4 cm x 4 cm	3 cm x 3 cm	2 cm x 2 cm	1 cm x 1 cm
No. of squares	1	4	9	16

I can construct 30 squares. 30 squares are similar.
There are 3 congruent groups.

Unit 4

1. Diagrams A and D illustrate a translation.
2. Diagrams B and C illustrate a reflection.
3. Diagrams B and D illustrate a rotation.
4. a. Translation   b. Reflection   c. Rotation
5. Suggested answer:

   It is a rotation.
6. It is a rotation.
7. a. A, D; C, E; F, G can match.
   b. B does not have a match.
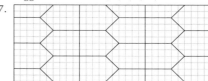
                                    (either one)
8.
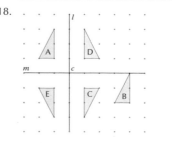
   a. 1   b. 2   c. 1
9. a. B and C have rotational symmetry.
   b. For figures B and C, a $\frac{1}{2}$ turn will rotate the object onto itself.
10. It has rotational symmetry.
11. It is 5.   12.   D, A, B, C, E.
13.

14. a. Ε,*,κ,Φ have a horizontal line of symmetry.
    b. *,Π,Φ,Ⅲ have a vertical line of symmetry.
    c. *,Φ have rotational symmetry.
15. A and E can.
16. Suggested answer: H, L, E, V, N, Z
17.

18.

19. a. The parallelograms all have an area of 4 square units.
    b. K to L ⟶ translated 4 right 1 down.
       K to M ⟶ rotated 180° about point x.
       K to N ⟶ reflected in the line l.
20.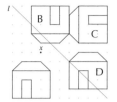

Challenge

1. Suggested answer:

2. Suggested answer:

   Yes. A figure with only one line of symmetry does not have rotational symmetry, e.g. an isosceles triangle.

Midway Review

1. a. Dimensions : 12 ÷ 100 by 12 ÷ 100 by 3 ÷ 100
       = 0.12 by 0.12 by 0.03
       The dimensions are 0.12 m by 0.12 m by 0.03 m (12 cm by 12 cm by 3 cm).
   b. Space : 12 x 12 x 3 = 432
       The space inside the model is 432 cm^3.
   c. Area : 12 x 12 x 2 + 12 x 3 x 2 + 12 x 3 x 2 = 432
       432 cm^2 of cardboard is needed.
   d. Scale : 1:100; No. of times bigger : 100 x 100 x 100 = 1000000
       The space occupied by the cottage is 1 000 000 times bigger than that of the model.
   e. Scale of the model : 1:100
       No. of times bigger : 100 x 100 = 10000
       The interior surface area of the cottage is 10 000 times bigger than that of the model.
   f. D
2. a. There are 9 triangles similar to △ABC.
   b. There are 3 triangles congruent to △ABD.
   c. Area : $\frac{8}{2}$ x $\frac{6}{2}$ = 12   The area is 12 cm^2.
   d. Area : ($\frac{6}{2}$ + 6) x $\frac{8}{2}$ ÷ 2 = 18   The area is 18 cm^2.
   e. Total surface area : 8.5 x 6 x 2 + (6 x 8 ÷ 2) x 2 = 150
       The total surface area is 150 cm^2.
   f. Total surface area : (6 x 8 ÷ 2) x 2 + 8.5 x 6 x 2 + 6 x 6 x 5
       = 48 + 102 + 180 = 330
       The total surface area is 330 cm^2.
   g. 12 2-cm cubes will have 2 painted faces.
   h. Height : 20 − $\frac{6 \times 6 \times 6}{10 \times 8}$ = 17.3
       The original height was 17.3 cm.
   i.

3. a. Area : 6 x 4 = 24   The area is 24 m^2.
   b. Area : (6 x 4) + (4 x 2.5 x 2) + (6 x 2.5 x 2) − (1 x 2) − (1 x 1) = 71
       The area is 71 m^2.

c. No. of tiles : 24 x 100 x 100 ÷ (25 x 25) = 384
   384 tiles are needed.
d. 1 box has 50 tiles; 8 boxes are needed for 384 tiles.
   Cost : 21.95 x 8 = 175.60   The cost is $175.60.
e. No. of tiles : 8 x 50 − 384 = 16   16 tiles are left over.
f. Total area to be painted = 71
   Amount of paint : 71 ÷ 4 x 2 = 35.5
   35.5 L of paint is needed.
g. No. of cans of paint needed : 35.5 ÷ 4 = 8.875 (9 cans)
   Cost : 27.99 x 9 = 251.91
   The cost of the paint is $251.91.
h. Amount of paint : 9 x 4 − 35.5 = 0.5
   0.5 L of paint will be left over.

4.
   Cut along the dotted lines   Cut into halves

   I would cut the cube diagonally first and then cut it into halves.
5. XY:8 = 2.4:4;   XY = $\frac{2.4 \times 8}{4}$ = 4.8
   ZY:5 = 2.4:4;   ZY = $\frac{2.4 \times 5}{4}$ = 3
   Perimeter of △XYZ : 2.4 + 4.8 + 3 = 10.2
   The perimeter of △XYZ is 10.2 cm.
6. I would not consider tile D because pentagons can't form a tiling pattern.
7.

   She could use some square-shaped bricks along with the octagon-shaped bricks to form the tiling pattern.
8.

   A 8, 8   B 0, 4   C 6, 6

Unit 5

1. a. B   b. D   c. A   2. C
3. a. The greatest increase was between 1995 and 1996.
   b. There was a decrease between 1993 and 1994.
   c. No. It was because a separate circle would be needed for each year.
   d. About 33% of female workers would be expected in the year 2002.
4. Graph A : The horizontal axis is not labelled and marked properly. It is meant to convey the trend of sales of ruby red wine.
   Graph B : The vertical scale should start at 0 and the title of the graph is inappropriate. It is meant to convey the number of absent employees in a week.
   Graph C : The scale along the horizontal axis is not consistent. It is meant to convey the trend of prices of 1 litre of gas in Ontario.
5. a. i. I would use graph B because it shows a steady increase in profits made by the company.
      ii. I would use graph C because the line showing the profits made by the drug company rises sharply from 1990 to 1999.
      iii. I would use graph A because the line showing the profits made by the drug company increases slowly from 1990 to 1999.
   b. The profit might be about 900 million dollars in 2000.

c. Profits made by the drug company between 1990 and 1999:

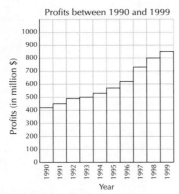

Profits between 1990 and 1999

6. a. 60°, 90°, 150°, 60°

b. Students' Activities

c. Suggested answer:
Bar graph or Pictograph

d. A line graph would not be suitable.

7. a.

tens	ones
3	7
4	8
5	0, 2, 8
6	4, 6, 7, 8
7	2, 5, 5, 9
8	3, 5, 9
9	1, 5

b.

Score	Frequency
30 - 39	1
40 - 49	1
50 - 59	3
60 - 69	4
70 - 79	4
80 - 89	3
90 - 99	2

c. Scores of Students

d. Scores of Students

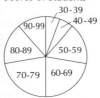

e. There are 18 students and 16 got 50 or more marks. The passing percentage of the students was $\frac{16}{18}$ x 100% = 88.9%.

Challenge

1. It reached its highest value in October and its lowest value in August.

2. Percentage change : $\frac{280 - 290}{290}$ x 100% = -3.45%
There was a decrease of 3.45%.

3. Percentage change : $\frac{340 - 250}{250}$ x 100% = 36%
There was an increase of 36%.

Unit 6

1. Suggested answers:
   a. 13, 16, 16   b. 15, 15, 21   c. 14, 15, 19
   d. 10, 14, 15   e. 15, 16, 16, 17   f. 6, 7, 8

2. a. Mean : (15 + 20 + 20 + 15 + 18 + 23 + 18 + 24 + 18) ÷ 9 = 19
   The mean is 19.
   b. Median : 15, 15, 18, 18, 18, 20, 20, 23, 24
   The median is 18 and the mode is 18.

c. Mean : (15 + 15 + 18 + 18 + 18 + 20 + 20 + 23 + 24 + 29) ÷ 10 = 20
Median : (18 + 20) ÷ 2 = 19
The mean would increase. The median would be the average of 18 and 20 instead of 18. The mode would not be affected.

3. a. Mean : (7 + 9 + 11 + 12 + 14x2 + 18 x 2 + 19 + 21 + 23 + 24 + 26x2 + 28x2 + 35x3 + 38x2 + 42x2) ÷ 23 = 563 ÷ 23 = 24.48
   The mean is 24.48.
   b. The median is 24. The mode is 35.

4. a. Mean : (30000x12 + 40000x2 + 45000x3 + 60000x2 + 100000) ÷ 20 = 39750   The mean is 39 750.
   The median is 30 000.   The mode is 30 000.
   b. I would use the mean because it is higher than the mode and the median. It would make the salary look more attractive.
   c. It would affect the mean but not the median or mode.
   d. The median or mode best represents the salaries because it is the most likely salary you would earn when you start working there.

5. Average : (1.25x5 + 1.25x3 + 0.95x4) ÷ 12
   = (6.25 + 3.75 + 3.8) ÷ 12 = 1.15
   The average price they paid was $1.15 per ice cream cone.

6. Mean : (25 + 32x2 + 24x3 + 28x4 + 0) ÷ 11 = 24.82
   The mean allowance of the children is $24.82.

7. The mean is 73.2. The median is 72. The range is 78 – 68 = 10.

8. a. The winning heights increased except in 1992.
   b. Height : (1.83 + 1.92 + 1.93 + 1.96 + 2.08 + 2.09 +2.07 + 2.15) ÷ 8 ≈ 2
   The approximate winning height is 2 m.
   c. If the trend continued, the height might be 2.16 m.
   d. Range : 2.15 – 1.83 = 0.32   The range is 0.32 m.

9. Average : (70 x 25 + 60 x 30) ÷ 55 = (1750 + 1800) ÷ 55 = 64.5
   The average percentage is 64.55.

10. Sum : 20 x 3 – 15 = 45   The sum of the other 2 numbers is 45.

11. a. Mean: (8 + 8 + 9 + 9 + 12 + 13 + 15 + 17 + 31) ÷ 9 = 13.56
    The mean is 13.56; the median is 12; the modes are 8 and 9.
    b. The mean best reflects the data because it is the average of all the data; the modes only show the most common values.
    c. I would use the mean to show how bad the problem was.
    d. I would use the mode since it could make the problem look less serious.

12. a. Average : (750 + 900 + 1000 + 1050 + 1100) ÷ 5 = 960
    The average sales are 960 million dollars ($960 000 000).
    b. This impression is created because the vertical scale does not start at zero, so it makes the increase look greater.

13. a. 104.68/sq. km;   334.22/sq. km;   225.59/sq. km;
    183.33/sq. km;   453.61/sq. km
    b. South Korea is the most densely populated country.
    c. Mean : (197 + 125 + 67 + 22 + 44) ÷ 5 = 91
    The mean population size is 91 millions (91 000 000).
    d. Put the data in order : 22, 44, 67, 125, 197
    The median population size is 67 millions.
    e. Bar graph. Here, 2 bar graphs would be appropriate --- one for population and one for area, or we may use 1 bar graph for population density.

Challenge

5 of the 7 test scores should be 34, 60, 70, 70 and 71.
The sum of the other 2 tests : 55 x 7 – (34 + 60 + 70 + 70 + 71) = 80
A. 34, 39, 41, 60, 70, 70, 71
B. 34, 38, 42, 60, 70, 70, 71
C. 34, 37, 43, 60, 70, 70, 71
D. 34, 36, 44, 60, 70, 70, 71
E. 34, 35, 45, 60, 70, 70, 71

Unit 7

1. a. $\frac{24}{50}$ (or $\frac{12}{25}$) of the flips turned up heads.

   b. There is no definite answer.

   c. She should expect heads to come up 250 times.

   d. $\frac{1}{2}$ of the flips should come up heads.

   e. The probability of getting heads is $\frac{1}{2}$.

   f. Yes, it is possible but it is unlikely to happen.

2.
   H $<$ H (H H) Carol
          T (H T) Debbie

   T $<$ H (T H) Debbie
          T (T T) Carol

   They are both likely to win because their chances of winning are the same.

3.
   H $<$ H $<$ H (H H H) Eric
              T (H H T) Frank
          T $<$ H (H T H) Frank
              T (H T T) Frank

   T $<$ H $<$ H (T H H) Frank
              T (T H T) Frank
          T $<$ H (T T H) Frank
              T (T T T) Eric

   Frank is likely to win.

4. a. Spinner A : P (3) = $\frac{1}{3}$

   Spinner B : P (3) = $\frac{1}{2}$

   Spinner C : P (3) = $\frac{1}{6}$

   b. Spinner A : He should expect 10 times.
      Spinner B : He should expect 15 times.
      Spinner C : He should expect 5 times.

   c. No, it doesn't depend on the number of spins.
   d. Spinner A.

5. a. It doesn't matter because the priority of guessing does not affect the probability of getting the right coloured ball.

   b. P (W) = $\frac{20}{60}$ = $\frac{1}{3}$ The probability is $\frac{1}{3}$.

   c. The most likely outcome is getting a black ball.

6. a. P (4) = $\frac{1}{6}$ The probability is $\frac{1}{6}$.

   b. P (5) = $\frac{1}{6}$; P (6) = $\frac{1}{6}$; P (>4) = $\frac{1}{6}$ + $\frac{1}{6}$ = $\frac{2}{6}$ = $\frac{1}{3}$
      The probability is $\frac{1}{3}$.

7. a. P (H) = $\frac{2}{8}$ or $\frac{1}{4}$

   The probability that there will be hamburgers for lunch is $\frac{1}{4}$.

   b. I would like her to use spinner B because the chance of getting spaghetti in spinner B is higher than that in spinner A.

   c. He should get 4 points because the probability of getting lasagna is half the probability of getting a hamburger.

8. a.

⊕	1	2	3	4	5	6
1	2	3	4	5	6	7
2	3	4	5	6	7	8
3	4	5	6	7	8	9
4	5	6	7	8	9	10
5	6	7	8	9	10	11
6	7	8	9	10	11	12

   b. No, they are not.

   c. P (4) = $\frac{3}{36}$ = $\frac{1}{12}$ The probability is $\frac{1}{12}$.

   d. P (7) = $\frac{6}{36}$ = $\frac{1}{6}$ 7 is most likely.

9. P (a double) = $\frac{6}{36}$ = $\frac{1}{6}$

   The probability of getting a double is $\frac{1}{6}$.

10. a. 48 different outcomes can only be obtained by rolling 2 dice with either 4 and 12 faces or 6 and 8 faces.
    Possible outcomes of 2 dice (the sum of 6) with 4 and 12 faces:
    (1, 5), (2, 4), (4, 2) and (3, 3)
    Possible outcomes of 2 dice (the sum of 6) with 6 and 8 faces:
    (1, 5), (5, 1), (2, 4), (4, 2) and (3, 3)
    Trish is using the dice with 6 and 8 faces.

    b. No. of possible outcomes : 48;
       Favourable outcomes : (6, 7), (5, 8)
       The probability is $\frac{2}{48}$ ($\frac{1}{24}$).

11. a. (Quebec, Montreal, Hull); (Quebec, Hull, Montreal); (Montreal, Quebec, Hull); (Montreal, Hull, Quebec); (Hull, Quebec, Montreal); (Hull, Montreal, Quebec).
    There are 6 different orders.

    b. No. It depends on where you start.

12. a. P (6) = $\frac{1}{6}$ x $\frac{1}{6}$ x $\frac{1}{6}$ = $\frac{1}{216}$ The probability is $\frac{1}{216}$.

    b. P (4) = $\frac{1}{216}$;   P (5) = $\frac{1}{216}$

       P (4 or 5) = $\frac{1}{216}$ + $\frac{1}{216}$ = $\frac{2}{216}$ ($\frac{1}{108}$)

       The probability is $\frac{1}{108}$.

    c. P (all match) = $\frac{6}{216}$ ($\frac{1}{36}$)   The probability is $\frac{1}{36}$.

13. P (6) = $\frac{1}{6}$ 10 times out of 60 will win.
    Money I win : 2 x 10 = 20
    I expect to win $20.00 by rolling the die 60 times.

14. a. All possible outcomes : {(1,2);(1,3);(1,4);(1,5);(2,1);(2,3);(2,4);(2,5); (3,1);(3,2);(3,4);(3,5);(4,1);(4,2);(4,3);(4,5);(5,1);(5,2);(5,3);(5,4)}
    The probability of getting both of them even is $\frac{2}{20}$ ($\frac{1}{10}$).

    b. No. of favourable outcomes : 12;
       No. of possible outcomes : 20
       The probability of getting one of them even is $\frac{12}{20}$ ($\frac{3}{5}$).

15. Possible outcomes : {AA; AB; AC; AB; AC; BC};   P (W) = $\frac{1}{6}$
    The probability that you will win is $\frac{1}{6}$.

Challenge
4CD = A, B, C, D.
Possible outcomes : {(A,B); (A,C); (A,D); (B,C); (B,D); (C, D)}
There are 6 different ways.

Final Review

1. D	2. C	3. B	4. D	5. C
6. B	7. C	8. B	9. A	10. D

11. Mean : (85 + 82 + 91 + 72 + 75 + 85) ÷ 6 = 81.67
    Median : (82 + 85) ÷ 2 = 83.5   Mode : 85
    Julie should choose the mode because it shows the highest score.

12. There are 2 possible ways :
    • To score 85 or more on the 3 tests
    • To score less than 85 on 1 test and 85 or more on the other 2 tests

13. Sum of the 3 upcoming tests :
    (80 x 9) − (85 + 82 + 91 + 72 + 75 + 85) = 230
    The sum of the scores on the 3 upcoming tests should be 230, e.g. 75, 75, 80.

14. A bar graph should be used because it shows the actual score on each test clearly.

15. There are two scores (72 and 75) equivalent to Grade B.
    P(70 – 79%) = $\frac{2}{6}$ = $\frac{1}{3}$ The probability is $\frac{1}{3}$.

16. The median of Julie's tests is 83.5. Mary should get 83 or below on 2 other tests, 84 on 1 test and 84 or above on the remaining tests.
    (e.g. 81, 82, 83, *84, 85, 86   *2nd test)

17. She should get more scores of 85 than other scores on her first 6 Math tests.

18. a. No. of hours : $\frac{30}{360}$ x 24 = 2

    A typical 12-year-old child spends 2 hours per day on homework.

    b. Sleeping : $\frac{120}{360}$ x 100% = 33.3%

    About 33.3% of a day is spent on sleeping.

    c. It shows how the day is divided up.

    d. Percentage on school and homework might increase.
    Percentage on eating and sleeping might decrease.

19. a. Total no. of chocolate bars : 500 x 20 = 10000

    Total no. of coupons : $\frac{10000}{50}$ + $\frac{10000}{200}$ = 200 + 50 = 250

    Fair distribution : $\frac{10000}{250}$ = 40

    Every 40 bars (2 boxes) should contain 1 of the 2 coupons.

    b. P (win) = $\frac{10}{40}$ = $\frac{1}{4}$ The probability is $\frac{1}{4}$.

    c. Cost : 200 x 0.8 x 0.5 + 50 x 0.8 x 2 = 80 + 80 = 160
    The total cost of the promotion is $160.00.

20. a. A

    B

    C

    The proportion of the colours on each spinner is based on the number of times they occured when Jane spun each of them 100 times.

    b.
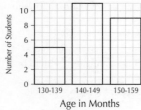
    H ⟨ H – H H
        T – H T

    T ⟨ H – T H
        T – T T

    P (H H) = $\frac{1}{4}$;   No. of times : 20 x $\frac{1}{4}$ = 5

    He should expect to win 5 times.

21. a.

tens	ones
13	5, 8, 8, 9, 9
14	0, 0, 0, 1, 2, 4, 4, 5, 6, 8, 9
15	0, 0, 0, 0, 1, 3, 6, 8, 9

    The median age is 145 months.

    b.   Ages of Grade 7 Students

(bar graph: Number of Students vs Age in Months; 130-139 ≈ 5, 140-149 = 11, 150-159 = 9)

22. a. JCBD, JCDB, JBCD, JBDC, JDCB, JDBC,
    CJBD, CJDB, CBJD, CBDJ, CDJB, CDBJ,
    BJCD, BJDC, BCJD, BCDJ, BDJC, BDCJ,
    DBJC, DBCJ, DJBC, DJCB, DCBJ, DCJB

    b. There are 24 different running orders.

    c. P(J) = $\frac{6}{24}$ = $\frac{1}{4}$ The probability is $\frac{1}{4}$.

    d. There are 6 different running orders.